# POETIC HOPE
# a 30-day Journal for women

*SIOBHAN MARIE*

Scriptures taken from the Holy Bible, New International Version®, NIV®.
Copyright © 1973, 1978, 1984, 2011 by Biblica, Inc.™ Used by permission of
Zondervan. All rights reserved worldwide. www.zondervan.com The "NIV" and
"New International Version" are trademarks registered in the United States Patent
and Trademark Office by Biblica, Inc.™

## Dedication

To my children, **Charlie, Jasmine** and **Levi** who have heard
much of this countless times before, in sermons, in day to day life
and deep family discussions. You make me want to stretch out
in faith one more time, and look forward, with great anticipation to
see all that God has prepared for each of you.

# Contents

# Acknowledgements

Thank you **Coll** for your constant belief in me and for motivating me to write.

Thank you **Cath** for never giving up on me and for inspiring me to live bigger.

Thank you **Liz** for bringing poetry back into my life and for showing up when I needed it most.

# Day 1

## Come as you are

She straightened her hair and smoothed out her dress
She whispered to no one, I feel such a mess

Will they see through me? I think they might
I think they'll know I got drunk Saturday night

They're all so perfect I can't keep up
I want to fit in but I'm not good enough

I heard about grace and forgiveness as well
I heard about second chances and starting again

What if it's my third or twentieth time round?
Can I still come and will mercy be found?

I'll be late, at the back, but I will show up
Lord forgive me and on me don't give up

Let us then approach God's throne of grace with confidence, so that
we may receive mercy and find grace to help us in our time of need.
*Hebrews 4:16*

Because of the Lord's great love we are not
consumed, for His compassions never fail. They
are new every morning; great is your faithfulness.
*Lamentations 3:22-23*

We all, like sheep, have gone astray, each
of us has turned to our own way; and the
Lord has laid on Him the iniquity of us all.
*Isaiah 53:6*

# Day 1 Reflection

**Thankful for:**

1.
_____

2.
_____

3.
_____

**Praying for:**

**Answers to Prayers:**

## Questions to ask ?

1. Why is it sometimes difficult to come to God?

2. When do you compare yourself with others?

3. What stops you being confident with God or in church?

## 3 truths to remember

saved - loved - chosen - called

# Day 2

## Words

Words hurt
Words heal
Words are false
Words are real

Words give
Words take
Words can fix
Words can break

Words
Words
Are only true
If you let them belong to you

Your Word is power
Your Word shifts
Your Word enables
Your Word lifts

Your word is a lamp for my feet,
a light on my path.
*Psalm 119:105*

Let the morning bring me word of your unfailing love,
for I have put my trust in you. Show me the way I
should go, for to you I entrust my life.
*Psalm 143:8*

For the word of God is alive and active. Sharper than any double-
edged sword, it penetrates even to dividing soul and spirit, joints
and marrow; it judges the thoughts and attitudes of the heart.
*Hebrews 4:12*

# Day 2 Reflection

**Thankful for:**

1. _____

2. _____

3. _____

**Praying for:**

**Answers to Prayers:**

## Questions to ask ?

1. When has someone hurt you with their words?

2. How careful are you with your words?

3. How can you apply God's Word in your life today?

## 3 truths to remember

saved - loved - chosen - called

# Day 3

## Mercy

Here I am
looking to you
knowing you give
Mercy
when I need it most.
Tired
from keeping it
together you give
Mercy
when I need it most.
You said come
I don't hesitate
boldly
I bow down.
Here
with You is
Mercy
when I need it most.

In him and through faith in Him we may
approach God with freedom and confidence.
*Ephesians 3:12*

I say to myself, "The Lord is my portion;
therefore I will wait for Him."
*Lamentations 3:24*

"Come to me, all you who are weary and burdened, and I will
give you rest. Take my yoke upon you and learn from me, for
I am gentle and humble in heart, and you will find rest for
your souls. For my yoke is easy and my burden is light."
*Matthew 11:28-30*

# Day 3 Reflection

**Thankful for:**

1.

2.

3.

**Praying for:**

**Answers to Prayers:**

## Questions to ask ?

1. What is it you need most from God today?

2. What burdens are you carrying that you should bring to God?

3. Take time to find rest in God today.

## 3 truths to remember

saved - loved - chosen - called

# Day 4

## Depression

I know you, we've met before
in the autumn of '96 when I was 22.
I walked the long leafy road to an aging care home
for an early shift at work.
It was already dark but you came over me like a wave,
silent, stealthy, grave.
I halted my steps in the darkest darkness
you feigned comfort but you were never my friend.
I had met you before
this was not the first time
nulling, deceiving, stealing my joy.
I waited a moment and held my breath
and worship came out in defiance and strength.
I know you, we've met before
but I get to choose
who comes through my door.
Not by myself, I'm weak on my own
Holy Spirit helper, I'm not alone.

Why, my soul, are you downcast?
Why so disturbed within me?
Put your hope in God,
for I will yet praise Him,
my Saviour and my God
*Psalm 42:11*

But you, Lord, are a shield around me,
my glory, the One who lifts my head high.
*Psalm 3:3*

Now the Lord is the Spirit, and where the
Spirit of the Lord is, there is freedom.
*2 Corinthians 3:17*

# Day 4 Reflection

**Thankful for:**

1.

_____

2.

_____

3.

_____

**Praying for:**

**Answers to Prayers:**

## Questions to ask ?

1. What things trigger sadness or low mood in you?

2. What can you praise God for, despite how you feel?

3. Speak God's Word into your soul and over your life today.

## 3 truths to remember

saved - loved - chosen - called

# Day 5

## Shepherd

You call me by name
You lead me out
I know _Your_ _voice._
You hem me in
behind and before
I know _Your_ _heart._
You bring me to
quiet still waters
I know _Your_ _rest._
You give me life
abundant and full
I know _Your_ _grace._
You walk with me
mountains and valleys
I know _Your_ _presence._

He makes me lie down in green pastures, He leads
me beside quiet waters, He refreshes my soul. He
guides me along the right paths for His name's sake.
_Psalm 23:2-3_

The gatekeeper opens the gate for him, and the sheep listen to his
voice. He calls his own sheep by name and leads them out. When he
has brought out all his own, he goes on ahead of them, and his sheep
follow him because they know his voice.
_John 10:3-4_

# Day 5 Reflection

**Thankful for:**

1.

2.

3.

**Praying for:**

**Answers to Prayers:**

## Questions to ask ?

1. In what ways do you hear God's voice?

2. Why is it sometimes hard to stop and rest with God?

3. When can you take time-out to listen to God today?

## 3 truths to remember

saved - loved - chosen - called

# Day 6

## Mind Games

See-saw up and down.
Swing swing back and forth.
A game I play
but never win
encore, encore
I'm holy and good.
I'm ungodly and bad.
Sometimes I'm happy.
Sometimes I'm sad.
I do the things I don't want to do.
I don't do the things I know I should do.
What do I want? that is the thing.
I want both but then I can't win.

Swing swing, back and forth.
See-saw, up and down.
Choose your side, live your life
for Jesus? For sin?
Don't give up now.
It hurts to fight
a battle like this.
Settle your mind
in there is bliss.

---

The mind governed by the flesh is death, but the mind
governed by the Spirit is life and peace.

*Romans 8:6*

We know that the law is spiritual; but I am unspiritual, sold as a slave to sin. I do not understand what I do. For what I want to do I do not do, but what I hate I do. And if I do what I do not want to do, I agree that the law is good. As it is, it is no longer I myself who do it, but it is sin living in me. For I know that good itself does not dwell in me, that is, in my sinful nature. For I have the desire to do what is good, but I cannot carry it out. For I do not do the good I want to do, but the evil I do not want to do—this I keep on doing. Now if I do what I do not want to do, it is no longer I who do it, but it is sin living in me that does it. So I find this law at work: Although I want to do good, evil is right there with me. For in my inner being I delight in God's law; but I see another law at work in me, waging war against the law of my mind and making me a prisoner of the law of sin at work within me. What a wretched man I am! Who will rescue me from this body that is subject to death? Thanks be to God, who delivers me through Jesus Christ our Lord! *Romans 7:14-25*

# Day 6 Reflection

**Thankful for:**

**1.**

_____

**2.**

_____

**3.**

_____

**Praying for:**

**Answers to Prayers:**

## Questions to ask ❓

1. What is the biggest battle in your mind?

2. How can you settle the issue with God?

3. What can you do today to keep your mind focused on God?

## 3 truths to remember

saved - loved - chosen - called

# Day 7

Finally, brothers and sisters, whatever is true, whatever is noble, whatever is right, whatever is pure, whatever is lovely, whatever is admirable—if anything is excellent or praiseworthy—think about such things.

*Philippians 4:8*

## Truth

*Mind* are you true?
Think on what is real not
escape to the unreal
it detracts from the beauty of today.
*Mind* don't limit the power of truth
its impact on faith, focus, friendship
by being untrue
True to you
True to God
True to the life you have been given.
*Mind* stay true
to God's Word which
spoken by you is the Amen to
activate its power in your life.
*Mind* go on a fast
Fast fake. Fast fear.
Fast negative thinking
and false ideas.
*Mind* is it right? Is it true?
Focus on Jesus
Your perpetual truth.

You will keep in perfect peace those whose minds are steadfast, because they trust in you. Trust in the Lord forever, for the Lord, the Lord Himself, is the Rock eternal.

*Isaiah 26:3-4*

13

# Day 7 Reflection

**Thankful for:**

**1.**
_____

**2.**
_____

**3.**
_____

**Praying for:**

**Answers to Prayers:**

## Questions to ask ?

1. What do you worry about the most and why?

2. What fantasies or unrealistic thoughts do you need to let go of, to be more thankful for today?

3. Which Bible verses will you use to replace negative thoughts today?

## 3 truths to remember

saved - loved - chosen - called

# Day 8

## To Hope

Hope you were with me
when I couldn't see
how to move forward
how to be me

Hope you were with me
as walls tumbled down
everything around me
fell to the ground

Hope you were kind
and taught me to see
that out of the rubble
I could be free

Hope show me tomorrow
let possibility unfold
of how we can rebuild
and a new story be told

Be joyful in hope, patient in affliction, faithful in prayer.
*Romans 12:12*

Therefore, since we have been justified through faith, we have peace with God through our Lord Jesus Christ, through whom we have gained access by faith into this grace in which we now stand. And we boast in the hope of the glory of God. Not only so, but we also glory in our sufferings, because we know that suffering produces perseverance; perseverance, character; and character, hope. And hope does not put us to shame, because God's love has been poured out into our hearts through the Holy Spirit, who has been given to us.
*Romans 5:1-5*

Be strong and take heart,
all you who hope in the Lord.
*Psalm 31:24*

# Day 8 Reflection

**Thankful for:**

**1.**
_____

**2.**
_____

**3.**
_____

**Praying for:**




**Answers to Prayers:**



## Questions to ask ?

1. What are 3 things you really hope for?

2. In what areas have you lost hope?

3. How can you be joyful in hope today?

## 3 truths to remember

saved - loved - chosen - called

# Day 9

## Time

Time is a healer, so they say
I don't believe it. Do you?
Time won't change what you went through.
Time can't take back what was done to you.
Time brings change within and without
how you progress is your way out.
Lonely, but not alone.

There is One who
walks with you
to help, to free
to restore, to bring peace.
He understands your heart
and sets your mind at ease
not with an answer to the why but with the
knowledge He is
always close by.
Lonely, but not alone
on this journey of your soul.

He has made everything beautiful in its time. He has
also set eternity in the human heart; yet no one can
fathom what God has done from beginning to end.
*Ecclesiastes 3:11*

Be strong and courageous. Do not be afraid or
terrified because of them, for the Lord your God goes
with you; He will never leave you nor forsake you.
*Deuteronomy 31: 6*

So do not fear, for I am with you;
do not be dismayed, for I am your God.
I will strengthen you and help you;
I will uphold you with my righteous right hand.
*Isaiah 41:10*

# Day 9 Reflection

**Thankful for:**

1.

2.

3.

**Praying for:**

**Answers to Prayers:**

## Questions to ask ?

1. What areas of your heart and soul need healing?

2. What person or thing can God help you with today?

3. Which Bible verses remind you that God is with you?

## 3 truths to remember

saved - loved - chosen - called

# Day 10

## Process

My confidence is in what you've done
In the work that you've begun
If it could happen overnight
Then everything would be alright!

My confidence is in what you do
Your work in me is always true
If it could be a little quicker
Then I'll feel more like a winner!

My confidence is in your vision
That your work comes to fruition
Everything happens in your perfect time
According to your will and your design

My confidence is in you
Because you know what to do
In every trial and every test
You know what is for the best

For my tomorrow and my today
I trust You Lord, have your way
You will complete the work in me
To display your love and your glory

---

Being confident of this, that He who began a
good work in you will carry it on to completion
until the day of Christ Jesus.
*Philippians 1:6*

For we are God's handiwork, created in
Christ Jesus to do good works, which
God prepared in advance for us to do.
*Ephesians 2:10*

# Day 10 Reflection

**Thankful for:**

1.

2.

3.

**Praying for:**

**Answers to Prayers:**

## Questions to ask ?

1. What process are you in right now?

2. What are you finding a challenge in this process?

3. Why do you sometimes find it hard to trust God with your future?

## 3 truths to remember

saved - loved - chosen - called

# Breathing Space

| What have I learned about myself over the past 10 days? | What have I learned about God over the past 10 days? |
| --- | --- |
| | |

**A Bible Verse to memorise:**

_____

_____

_____

_____

_____

**In my heart and mind I have overcome:**

**Blessings I have experienced:**

| What I am still believing God for: | What I am still working on in myself: |
| --- | --- |
| | |

**A Bible Verse that gives me hope:**

_____

_____

_____

_____

_____

**A letter to my future self:**

**People I am praying for:**

# Day 11

## Broken

I broke my arm at 8
no lasting damage although I remember the pain
She broke my faith in people
my whole childhood I cant forget the fear, the shame
He broke my trust at 26
two decades of trying to cover the cracks
They broke my confidence at 33 the sting of the tears,
the tear in my heart, it all comes back
Is it me? Did I do something wrong? Or simply allow
others to string me along?
When did I give control of my heart, my emotions, my
innermost part for others to use and callously discard?
Always beside me was One who took care
of every emotion, joy and despair
Jesus covered, repaired and reset
so I could keep going and rework my mindset
Learning to guard and cover my heart
I am still discovering this intricate art
Broken, I have been
but also made whole
and now, for always
it is well with my soul

The Lord is close to the brokenhearted
and saves those who are crushed in spirit.
*Psalm 34:18*

He heals the brokenhearted
and binds up their wounds.
*Psalm 147:3*

Above all else, guard your heart, for everything you do flows from it.
*Proverbs 4:23*

# Day 11 Reflection

**Thankful for:**

**1.**

_____

**2.**

_____

**3.**

_____

**Praying for:**

**Answers to Prayers:**

## Questions to ask ?

1. How often are your feelings set by others?

2. What does it mean to guard your heart?

3. What can you learn about God through these verses today?

## 3 truths to remember

saved - loved - chosen - called

# Day 12

## Hope

I hoped in a husband
I hoped in wealth
I hoped in my job
I hoped in health
I hoped in clothes, make-up and hair
I found nothing valuable there
I hoped in success, achievements and fame
that didn't work... try again?!
I hoped in hard work and busy days
an endless treadmill, a meaningless parade
I hoped in a future, full and bright
it just seemed too far from sight
and so at last
what I knew to do
was bring all my hope
and give it to you
You promise not to hurt my heart
You promise no disappointment from the start
You promise an anchor for my soul
I lean in with hope, and I am made whole

May the God of hope fill you with all joy and peace as
you trust in Him, so that you may overflow with hope
by the power of the Holy Spirit.
*Romans 15:13*

We have this hope as an anchor for the soul, firm and
secure. It enters the inner sanctuary behind the curtain.
*Hebrews 6:19*

And hope does not put us to shame, because God's love has been poured
out into our hearts through the Holy Spirit, who has been given to us.
*Romans 5:5*

# Day 12 Reflection

**Thankful for:**

1.

_____

2.

_____

3.

_____

**Praying for:**




**Answers to Prayers:**




## Questions to ask ?

1. What are you hopeful in today?

2. When have you felt disappointed in things you hoped for?

3. Ask God for His joy and peace as you hope in Him today.

## 3 truths to remember

saved - loved - chosen - called

## Day 13

### Hurt

I don't feel like love, do you?
But I really don't like hate.
Sadness, sorrow
is all I can manage
in my current state

Do you think anyone can understand the emotions
tearing through your mind each day? Like a commuter train speeding with routine
thoughtlessness. Fear, hurt, shame, they move relentlessly.
Do they know the loss, the pain of expectations torn away? What tomorrow?

I hear their voices
the women past
told me of
undeserved angst
I listened but I never heard
experiences beyond
my own
but now I wish
I'd understood
for now I'm here
in the unknown

Dear friend you are not
on your own
although it's harder
than ever before.
I pray for you
I don't know your name
but dear friend I know
your pain.

Stay the course
a spacious place
awaits
as you put your trust
in the Lord's name

I love you, Lord, my strength. The Lord is my rock, my fortress and my deliverer; my God is my rock, in whom I take refuge, my shield and the horn of my salvation, my stronghold.
*Psalm 18:1-2*

You turned my wailing into dancing; you removed my sackcloth and clothed me with joy, that my heart may sing your praises and not be silent. Lord my God, I will praise you forever.
*Psalm 30:11-12*

He brought me out into a spacious place; He rescued me because He delighted in me.
*Psalm 18:19*

# Day 13 Reflection

**Thankful for:**

1.

2.

3.

**Praying for:**

**Answers to Prayers:**

## Questions to ask ❓

1. Bring any hurt you have to the Lord today.

2. How does God help you keep moving forward?

3. Pray for someone else who is dealing with hurt today.

## 3 truths to remember

saved - loved - chosen - called

# Day 14

## Forgiveness

Forgiving doesn't right a wrong
it makes you strong
Forgiving isn't giving in
giving up your right to feel
to hurt, to lash out,
grieved by sin.
Forgive to let go
the shock, the anger
Forgive so the
days don't get darker.
No one's getting off the hook
but your heart
is no longer shook
crushing, wrenching at you inside
live on the other side.
There might be a limp, a scar
but you have come too far
for someone who's no one
to limit what's ahead
live without dread.
Don't taint memories with revenge
this is not for you to avenge
don't carry hatred
it eats away at you
don't give that person
one more day of you.
Your future, your life
your freedom
seems impossible
help Holy Spirit
we need you in on it.
Power, strength
wisdom, grace
freedom because of the price that You paid.
Let them go,
Jesus knows.

> And when you stand praying, if you hold anything against anyone, forgive them, so that your Father in heaven may forgive you your sins.
> Mark 11:25

> Praise the Lord, my soul, and forget not all His benefits— who forgives all your sins and heals all your diseases, who redeems your life from the pit and crowns you with love and compassion.
> *Psalm 103:2-4*

# Day 14 Reflection

**Thankful for:**

1.

_____

2.

_____

3.

_____

**Praying for:**

**Answers to Prayers:**

## Questions to ask ?

1. Who do you need to forgive today?

2. How do you feel about the process of forgiveness?

3. Why is it important to let go of hate and unforgiveness?

## 3 truths to remember

saved - loved - chosen - called

# Day 15

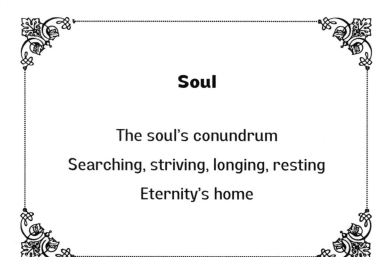

## Soul

The soul's conundrum

Searching, striving, longing, resting

Eternity's home

For the wages of sin is death, but the gift of God is
eternal life in Christ Jesus our Lord.
*Romans 6:23*

For God so loved the world that he gave his one and
only Son, that whoever believes in Him shall not perish
but have eternal life.
*John 3:16*

For our light and momentary troubles are achieving for us an eternal
glory that far outweighs them all. So we fix our eyes not on what is seen,
but on what is unseen, since what is seen is temporary, but what is
unseen is eternal
2 Corinthians 4:17-18

# Day 15 Reflection

**Thankful for:**

1. _____

2. _____

3. _____

**Praying for:**




**Answers to Prayers:**




## Questions to ask ?

1. Why is it important to keep focused on what is ' unseen'?

2. How can you think about eternity in your daily life?

3. Pray for a friend or family member who needs Jesus today.

## 3 truths to remember

saved - loved - chosen - called

# Day 16

"For I know the plans I have for you,"declares the Lord, "plans to prosper you and not to harm you, plans to give you hope and a future."
*Jeremiah 29:11*

---

Let us not become weary in doing good, for at the proper time we will reap a harvest if we do not give up.
*Galatians 6:9*

## In-between

Unsettled quiet
Like a dark country lane
Unfamiliar
Passing strangers
Searching for a friendly face
Unrecognised
You are on this road alone.
Step by step
No shortcut
Your narrow path to walk.

Misunderstood
Like rhetorical questions
Misrepresented
Pressing thoughts
Searching for answers
Unanswerable
You go unheard.
Day by day
No quitting
You have to walk on.

Unwelcome isolation
Like deserted ruins
Unknown
Hoping for time
To heal and restore
Unending
You heart holds on.
Prayer by prayer
No doubt
You find strength to walk.

Light will break through
As sunshine breaks the cloud
Hope will endure
As winter turns to spring.
March on my soul
March on

He gives strength to the weary and increases the power of the weak. Even youths grow tired and weary, and young men stumble and fall; but those who hope in the Lord will renew their strength. They will soar on wings like eagles; they will run and not grow weary, they will walk and not be faint.
*Isaiah 40:29-31*

# Day 16 Reflection

**Thankful for:**

1.

_____

2.

_____

3.

_____

**Praying for:**

**Answers to Prayers:**

## Questions to ask ?

1. What are you believing God for right now?

2. Why is the time between promise and fulfilment so challenging?

3. Where do you need to ask for strength and courage today?

## 3 truths to remember

saved - loved - chosen - called

# Day 17

## Valley

You are behind me
You stay beside me
You go before me
There is a way
through this valley

The darkest night before the dawn
You promise I will not fall
I'm in Your hands
When I can't see the way ahead
I turn to Your word instead
You surround me

My soul sings
Jesus my king
I lift my hands
and shout your praise
Jesus protector of my days

You are behind me
You stay beside me
You go before me
There is a way
through this valley

Even though I walk through the darkest valley, I will fear no evil, for you are with me; your rod and your staff, they comfort me. You prepare a table before me in the presence of my enemies. You anoint my head with oil; my cup overflows. Surely your goodness and love will follow me all the days of my life, and I will dwell in the house of the Lord forever.

*Psalm 23:4-6*

# Day 17 Reflection

**Thankful for:**

1.

_____

2.

_____

3.

_____

**Praying for:**

**Answers to Prayers:**

## Questions to ask ❓

1. What valley have you found yourself in?

2. How did King David speak about the 'valley'?

3. Where can you see God's goodness and love in your life today?

## 3 truths to remember

saved - loved - chosen - called

# Day 18

## Sowing

I cried. I sowed.
I sowed. I cried.
In the dark
Unknown

I sowed. I cried
I cried. I sowed.
You see me Lord
To You I'm known

Hour by hour
Day by day
Pressing on
Lord have Your way

And all at once
light breaks
darkness dissipates
standing in an open space
overwhelmed by your grace

Those who sow with tears will reap with songs of joy.
Those who go out weeping, carrying seed to sow,
will return with songs of joy, carrying sheaves with them.
*Psalm 126:5-6*

If I say, "Surely the darkness will hide me and the light become
night around me," even the darkness will not be dark to you;
the night will shine like the day, for darkness is as light to you.
*Psalm 139:11-12*

Sow your seed in the morning, and at evening let your hands
not be idle, for you do not know which will succeed, whether
this or that, or whether both will do equally well
*Ecclesiastes 11:6*

# Day 18 Reflection

**Thankful for:**

1.
_____

2.
_____

3.
_____

**Praying for:**

**Answers to Prayers:**

## Questions to ask ?

1. How is your attitude when you can't see the result of your faithfulness?

2. How do you keep sowing when life gets hard'?

3. What is God teaching you in the hidden season?

## 3 truths to remember

saved - loved - chosen - called

# Day 19

For the revelation awaits an appointed time; it speaks of the
end and will not prove false. Though it linger, wait for it; it
will certainly come and will not delay

*Habakkuk 2:3*

## Wait
Wait
Don't rush
I know you want to
Wait
Don't hurry
Although it's tempting
Wait for the Lord
Be strong and take heart
He's leading
He's guiding
Wait
You'll get there

We wait in hope for the Lord; He is our help and our shield. In
Him our hearts rejoice, for we trust in His holy name. May your
unfailing love be with us, Lord, even as we put our hope in you.

*Psalm 33:20-22*

Wait for the Lord; be strong and take heart and wait for the Lord

*Psalm 27:14*

# Day 19 Reflection

**Thankful for:**

1.

2.

3.

**Praying for:**

**Answers to Prayers:**

## Questions to ask ?

1. How do you treat others when you are waiting on the Lord?

2. How can you prepare well in the wait?

3. What are you learning about God as you wait on Him?

## 3 truths to remember

saved - loved - chosen - called

# Day 20

## Love

Love me
in my pjs and
ponytail hair.
Love me
in high heels or
in sports wear.
Love me
on the good days and
the bad days too.
Love me
when I'm winning and
when I'm failing too.
Love beyond the feelings
Love beyond the walls
the love I found in Jesus
lifts me when I fall.
When betrayed and abandoned
You stayed by my side
cover me under the shadow
of your wings where I can hide.
Not in shame and misery
but in faith, hope and love.
You are my protector
my gentle, patient dove.

For I am convinced that neither death nor life, neither angels nor demons, neither the present nor the future, nor any powers, neither height nor depth, nor anything else in all creation, will be able to separate us from the love of God that is in Christ Jesus our Lord.
*Romans 8:38-39*

Love is patient, love is kind. It does not envy, it does not boast, it is not proud. It does not dishonour others, it is not self-seeking, it is not easily angered, it keeps no record of wrongs. Love does not delight in evil but rejoices with the truth. It always protects, always trusts, always hopes, always perseveres.
*1 Corinthians 13:4-7*

# Day 20 Reflection

**Thankful for:**

**1.**

_____

**2.**

_____

**3.**

_____

**Praying for:**

**Answers to Prayers:**

## Questions to ask ?

1. How have you responded to betrayal and hurt?

2. When have you not loved someone as they are?

3. How can you grow in God's love today?

## 3 truths to remember

saved - loved - chosen - called

# Breathing Space

| What have I learned about myself over the past 10 days? | What have I learned about God over the past 10 days? |
|---|---|
|  |  |

**A Bible Verse to memorise:**

_____

_____

_____

_____

**In my heart and mind I have overcome:**



**Blessings I have experienced:**

| What I am still believing God for: | What I am still working on in myself: |
| --- | --- |
| | |

**A Bible Verse that gives me joy:**

_____

_____

_____

_____

_____

**A letter to someone I need to forgive:**

**People I am praying for:**

# Day 21

## Masks

Ellen Melon Muffin Pie
was taught to laugh and not to cry
to do what grown ups said she should
no question if it's bad or good

Ellen Melon Muffin Pie
learnt to smile and hide a lie
no one wants to know for real
what you need or how you feel

Ellen Melon Muffin Pie
knows pleasing others gets her by
Sundays you are good and clean
no matter how your week has been

Ellen wants to change her name
to live in truth and start again
Ellen knows she can be free
from a messed up history

Ellen decides to turn the page
it's her time for centre stage
no more lies and fear and doubt
faith in Jesus brought her out

Then you will know the truth, and the truth will set you free.
*John 8:32*

It is for freedom that Christ has set us free. Stand firm, then, and do not let
yourselves be burdened again by a yoke of slavery
*Galatians 5:1*

The thief comes only to steal and kill and destroy; I have come that they may have
life, and have it to the full.
*John 10:10*

# Day 21 Reflection

**Thankful for:**

**1.**

**2.**

**3.**

**Praying for:**

**Answers to Prayers:**

## Questions to ask ?

1. Are there times you didn't feel able to be yourself?

2. How can you be free from negative things in your past?

3. How can Jesus help you overcome fear and doubt?

## 3 truths to remember

saved - loved - chosen - called

# Day 22

## Dream

Dream dream and dream some more
discover what you were born for.
A dream can birth a new day
you work, you hope, you pray.

Dream when you're young
dream when you're old.
Forget the doubters
with imaginary powers.

Dream day and night
dream with all of your might.
God can do more than you ask or imagine
look to Him and he'll make it happen.

Dreamer dream on.
Don't let today
get in the way.

Now to Him who is able to do immeasurably more than all we ask or
imagine, according to His power that is at work within us.
*Ephesians 3:20*

And afterward, I will pour out my Spirit on all people.
Your sons and daughters will prophesy, your old men will
dream dreams, your young men will see visions.
*Joel 2:28*

Delight yourself in the Lord, and He will give you the desires of your heart.
*Psalm 37:4*

# Day 22 Reflection

**Thankful for:**

**1.** _____

**2.** _____

**3.** _____

**Praying for:**



**Answers to Prayers:**

## Questions to ask ?

1. What God dream do you have?

2. Have you ever given up on a God-given dream?

3. Ask the Holy Spirit to fill you afresh today with His ideas and inspiration.

## 3 truths to remember

saved - loved - chosen - called

# Day 23

## Expectations

It's all about how you look
on Instagram and Facebook
not too happy not too sad
don't want anyone feeling bad

Wear your smile with trendy clothes
look the part for the front row
don't bring doubt or worry here
no leader has anxiety or fear

Keeping up with the Jones'
making small talk, iPhones
sit at tables of high importance
your value is found in this performance

You won't fit in
if you don't look right
you won't fit in
if your dress is too tight
you won't find acceptance here
unless you cover up your fear

You won't find you
without being true
to who God made you
leave the haters
leave the fake
let it go
your future is at stake

> So then, just as you received Christ Jesus as Lord, continue to live your lives in Him, rooted and built up in Him, strengthened in the faith as you were taught, and overflowing with thankfulness.
> *Colossians 2:6-7*

> We played the pipe for you, and you did not dance; we sang a dirge, and you did not mourn.
> *Matthew 11:17*

Yes, my soul, find rest in God; my hope comes from him. Truly he is my rock and my salvation; he is my fortress, I will not be shaken. My salvation and my honor depend on God; he is my mighty rock, my refuge. Trust in him at all times, you people; pour out your hearts to him, for God is our refuge.

*Psalm 62:5-8*

# Day 23 Reflection

**Thankful for:**

**1.**
_____

**2.**
_____

**3.**
_____

**Praying for:**




**Answers to Prayers:**



## Questions to ask ?

1. How have the expectations of others affected you?

2. Why do we sometimes change to fit in with others?

3. How can you find your security and confidence in God today?

## 3 truths to remember

saved - loved - chosen - called

# Day 24

## Boundaries

No hope for her
a shake of the head

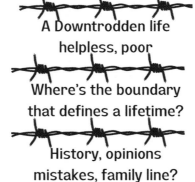

Her mind is too messed up
they said

Broken, hopeless
insecure

A Downtrodden life
helpless, poor

Where's the boundary
that defines a lifetime?

History, opinions
mistakes, family line?

Who allocates your
earthly zone?

Not him, not them,
but God alone

Safe and secure in
borders set by you

Expansive, exciting, endless
experiences to pursue

Lord, you alone are my portion and my cup; you make my lot secure. The boundary
lines have fallen for me in pleasant places; surely I have a delightful inheritance.

*Psalm 16:5-6*

For we are God's handiwork, created in Christ Jesus to do
good works, which God prepared in advance for us to do.

*Ephesians 2:10*

# Day 24 Reflection

**Thankful for:**

1. 

2. 

3. 

**Praying for:**

**Answers to Prayers:**

## Questions to ask ?

1. What has caused you to feel limited in life?

2. How can you change your mindset to see God's possibilities?

3. Write a list of limits that have been placed on you in your life, then write a promise from the Bible next to each one.

## 3 truths to remember

saved - loved - chosen - called

# Day 25

## No Worries

Worry worry
On my mind
Which is the biggest
Burden of all?
Saving Grace
Protects my mind
Jesus Jesus
Freedom from all

Fear fear
In my heart
What has the strongest
Grip of all?
Peace peace
Covers my heart
Jesus Jesus
Is bigger than all

Anxious anxious
Moments I face
Who is the person
I must please most?
Love love
Surrounds my life
Jesus Jesus
The one I live for

Do not be anxious about anything, but in every situation, by prayer and petition, with thanksgiving, present your requests to God. And the peace of God, which transcends all understanding, will guard your hearts and your minds in Christ Jesus.
*Philippians 4:6-7*

So do not worry, saying, 'What shall we eat?' or 'What shall we drink?' or 'What shall we wear?' For the pagans run after all these things, and your heavenly Father knows that you need them. But seek first his kingdom and his righteousness, and all these things will be given to you as well. Therefore do not worry about tomorrow, for tomorrow will worry about itself. Each day has enough trouble of its own.
*Matthew 6:31-34*

# Day 25 Reflection

**Thankful for:**

1.

2.

3.

**Praying for:**

**Answers to Prayers:**

**Questions to ask ?**

1. Why do we often not bring our worries to Jesus?

2. What situations make you anxious or afraid?

3. How can God help in these situations?

**3 truths to remember**

saved - loved - chosen - called

# Day 26

## ID

Who are you? Do you have ID?
I was Bullock but not anymore
I used to be Daly but that was before
I'm a mum, a daughter and a sister too
I'm also a friend and a cousin it's true.
At home I'm mum, at school Mrs B
I'm a customer at Lidl, there's not much more to me
I was a PA, a pastor, a leader
a creative director... I'm an avid reader.
At church I attend , for my children's spiritual health
I sit at the back and try to blend.
Who am I?
How am I known?
I'm no one really
I'm a bit on my own.
The Lord calls me chosen, saved and redeemed
a crown of splendour, royalty, esteemed
He said that He'll give me a brand new name
and then I will never be the same.
Is that just for once
when you are first saved?
I find that it happens
time and again
for life comes in seasons it ebbs and flows
Jesus knows the highs and lows.
He calls me His own
again and again
especially when I've forgotten
my name

> Before I formed you in the womb I knew you, before you were born I set you apart
> *Jeremiah 1:5*

For you created my inmost being; you knit me together in my mother's womb. I praise you because I am fearfully and wonderfully made; your works are wonderful, I know that full well. My frame was not hidden from you when I was made in the secret place, when I was woven together in the depths of the earth. Your eyes saw my unformed body; all the days ordained for me were written in your book before one of them came to be.

*Psalm 139:13-16*

# Day 26 Reflection

**Thankful for:**

1. _____

2. _____

3. _____

**Praying for:**

**Answers to Prayers:**

## Questions to ask ?

1. What labels do you have in your life?

2. Have the perceptions of others helped or held you back?

3. How does it help knowing how God sees you?

## 3 truths to remember

saved - loved - chosen - called

# Day 27

## Unwavering

I *remember* your faithfulness
in the midst of my pain
I *rejoice* in your goodness
again and again
I *repent* of my mistakes
I'm forgiven and saved
I *resolve* to speak truth
from every promise you gave

Blessed are those whose strength is in you, whose hearts are set on pilgrimage. As they pass through the Valley of Baka, they make it a place of springs; the autumn rains also cover it with pools. They go from strength to strength, till each appears before God in Zion.

*Psalm 84:5-7*

---

I will remember the deeds of the Lord; yes, I will remember your miracles of long ago. I will consider all your works and meditate on all your mighty deeds. Your ways, God, are holy. What god is as great as our God?

*Psalm 77:11-13*

---

For the Lord God is a sun and shield; the Lord bestows favour and honour; no good thing does He withhold from those whose walk is blameless.

*Psalm 84:11*

# Day 27 Reflection

**Thankful for:**

1. 

2. 

3. 

**Praying for:**

**Answers to Prayers:**

## Questions to ask ?

1. Consider the steps: Remember, Rejoice, Repent, Resolve...
How does this help you reflect on God's presence in your life today?

2. Where have you seen God at work?

3. How can you be more mindful of God during the day?

## 3 truths to remember

saved - loved - chosen - called

# Day 28

## Noble

I am ready for a noble task
Lord send me
to help, to preach, to pioneer, to teach.
PRAY
Oh yes dear Lord I'll pray on the way.
PRAY
And what else? There must be more.
Are you available to PRAY?
For your husband
For your family
For your friends
You don't need to be a hero
and try to save the world
to stand before a crowd
visible and known.
You can save your family in prayer;
Salvation - Wisdom - Protection
Freedom - Purpose - Strength
Break down generational strongholds.
Break the lie of the enemy.

Are you still ready for a noble task
although it is unseen?
Is there time available in your busy day?
PRAY

---

Do not be anxious about anything, but in every situation, by prayer and petition, with thanksgiving, present your requests to God.

*Philippians 4:6*

And pray in the Spirit on all occasions with all kinds of prayers and requests. With this in mind, be alert and always keep on praying for all the Lord's people.

*Ephesians 6:18*

In the same way, the Spirit helps us in our weakness. We do not know what we ought to pray for, but the Spirit himself intercedes for us through wordless groans.

*Romans 8:26*

# Day 28 Reflection

**Thankful for:**

1.

_____

2.

_____

3.

_____

**Praying for:**

**Answers to Prayers:**

## Questions to ask ?

1. Why are we sometimes too busy to pray?

2. How confident and useful do you feel when you pray for others?

3. Pray the Word of God over your family and friends today.

## 3 truths to remember

saved - loved - chosen - called

# Day 29

## Unfinished Purpose

What use am I
anymore?
Closed doors
Broken walls

What use am I
anyway?
No voice
No platform

What use am I
anywhere?
Backstreets
Side roads

Whose am I
always?
The Lord's
The Lord's

> I know that you can do all things; no purpose of yours can be thwarted.
> *Job 42:2*

Where do I belong
forever?
With Jesus
With Jesus

> Many are the plans in a person's heart, but it is the Lord's purpose that prevails
> *Proverbs 19:21*

What can I do
today?
Praise Him
Praise Him

But you are a chosen people, a royal priesthood, a holy nation,
God's special possession, that you may declare the praises of Him
who called you out of darkness into His wonderful light.
1 Peter 2:9

# Day 29 Reflection

**Thankful for:**

1.

2.

3.

**Praying for:**

**Answers to Prayers:**

## Questions to ask ?

1. When have you felt like you have lost your purpose?

2. Remind yourself of God's call and purpose for you.

3. Memorise one of today's Bible verses and speak it out over your life throughout the day.

## 3 truths to remember

saved - loved - chosen - called

# Day 30

## Presence

You give me all your attention
When the whole world is gone
What can I bring before you
Not even a song
I have no words to describe
How overwhelmed I feel
Sitting here with You
Your presence is so real
I can only say
Thank you
Thank you again and again
I hear an audience of angels
Singing 'Hallelujah to the King'

You make known to me the path of life; you
will fill me with joy in your presence, with
eternal pleasures at your right hand
*Psalm 16:11*

Praise the Lord. Praise the Lord from the heavens; praise him in the heights above. Praise him, all his angels; praise him, all his heavenly hosts. Praise him, sun and moon; praise him, all you shining stars. Praise him, you highest heavens and you waters above the skies. Let them praise the name of the Lord, for at his command they were created, and he established them for ever and ever— he issued a decree that will never pass away. Praise the Lord from the earth, you great sea creatures and all ocean depths, lightning and hail, snow and clouds, stormy winds that do his bidding, you mountains and all hills, fruit trees and all cedars, wild animals and all cattle, small creatures and flying birds, kings of the earth and all nations, you princes and all rulers on earth, young men and women, old men and children. Let them praise the name of the Lord, for his name alone is exalted; his splendour is above the earth and the heavens. And he has raised up for his people a horn, the praise of all his faithful servants, of Israel, the people close to his heart.
Praise the Lord.
Psalm 148

# Day 30 Reflection

**Thankful for:**

**1.** _____

**2.** _____

**3.** _____

**Praying for:**




**Answers to Prayers:**



## Questions to ask ?

1. How would you describe God's presence?

2. Take time for God to fill you with joy today.

3. Write your own Psalm/Poem/Song about Jesus.

## 3 truths to remember

saved - loved - chosen - called

# Breathing Space

| What have I learned about myself over the past 10 days? | What have I learned about God over the past 10 days? |
|---|---|
| | |

## A Bible Verse to memorise:

_____

_____

_____

_____

_____

**In my heart and mind I have overcome:**

**Blessings I have experienced:**

| What I am still believing God for: | What I am still working on in myself: |
| --- | --- |
| | |

## A Bible Verse that gives me courage:

_____

_____

_____

_____

_____

**A prayer to Jesus:**

**People I am praying for:**

*Thank you for joining me on this journey of hope and freedom.*
*I pray that your time with God has been helpful in building*
*your faith and giving you courage for each day.*
*Keep on keeping on. Siobhan*

## A PRAYER for you

**Lord Jesus,**
**Thank you for your Word and the truth that you bring to our lives.**
**For the person reading this right now, I pray you would bring**
**peace into their heart and mind. I thank you for your promise, that**
**you are always present and that you never fail.**
**We pray over every situation that they are facing today and**
**declare that you will work all things together for their good. Thank**
**you God that your ways are higher than our ways, and your**
**thoughts are higher than our thoughts. We trust you.**
**We bring any confusion, or any questions to you now and ask for**
**clarity through your Word. We pray for Holy Spirit boldness as we**
**live each day for you. Let each person grow in the knowledge that**
**you are for us and that your love never gives up on us.**
**For my friend here today, let your presence bring joy and freedom**
**from all worry, anxiety and fear. Let faith rise in their spirit, in the**
**mighty name of Jesus.**
**Amen**

*To become a Christian you can start with a prayer, like the one below.*
*You can pray yourself or with a friend..*

## PRAYER to become a Christian.

**Lord Jesus,**
**Thank you that you love me,**
**thank you that you are a good God.**
**Thank you that you died for me and rose again,**
**so that I can be saved and sure of eternity in Heaven.**
**I ask you today for all of the things that I need,**
**thank you that you provide for me.**
**Forgive me Jesus for all of the wrong things I have done,**
**thank you for your forgiveness, I accept it now.**
**Jesus, I would like you to be my Lord,**
**my saviour and my friend.**
**Please come into my heart and my life.**
**I surrender all that I am and all that I will be, to you.**
**Amen**

*What to do next:*
- *tell a Christian friend or Pastor about your decision and the prayer that you prayed, so they can pray with you and support you.*
- *read a verse or chapter from the Bible each day - the You Version Bible is a good place to start if you want to read the Bible on your phone..*
- *look for a church near you where you can go to a church service and meet other Christians. Do a google search of your area.*
- *talk to God each day so you can get to know Him more.*

Printed in Great Britain
by Amazon

2665a828-e71e-4e5f-9cd4-a77db41a1033R01